First published in Sweden by

Natur & Kultur

PO Box 27323

102 54 Stockholm, Sweden

First published in the United States of America by

Quarry Books, a member of

Quarto Publishing Group USA Inc.

100 Cummings Center

Suite 406-L

Beverly, Massachusetts 01915-6101

Telephone: (978) 282-9590

Fax: (978) 283-2742

www.quarrybooks.com

Visit www.Craftside.net for a behind-the-scenes peek at our crafty world!

ISBN: 978-1-63159-025-2

Digital edition published in 2015

eISBN: 978-1-62788-329-0

10 9 8 7 6 5 4 3 2 1

Photography: Maria Wretblad

Design: Katy Kimbell

Editorial staff: Maria Nilsson and Elisabeth Fock

Photo credits: Maria Wretblad: Cover and pp. 5-7, 116–117 and FoE (back).

Helena Karlsson: FoE (front), pp. 102–103 and 115.

Fideli Sundqvist: pp. 18–19, 82–84, 87, 96, and 98.

Martin Ridne: p 8. Magnus Cramer: pp. 124–125

Stylists: Saša Antic: pp. 42–47, 71, 73, 77 and Joanna Lavén: pp 59–61

English Translation: UMass Translation Center

Printed in China

PAPER

FIDELI SUNDQVIST

PHOTOGRAPHY **MARIA WRETBLAD**

Quarry Books
100 Cummings Center, Suite 406L
Beverly, MA 01915

quarrybooks.com • www.craftside.net

contents

preface:

From the time I was a child, I have had the opportunity to live close to enthusiastic people who were creative themselves. At home and in my mom's ceramics workshop there were materials and tools that I was free to use.

The first time I came into contact with paper as an art form was when my brother came home from Beijing with a couple of Chinese paper cutouts. The red dragons and flowers were cut from rice paper and were held together only by millimeter-thin lines. I was quite taken and amazed by the handiwork and patience that were behind these detailed cutouts. That was how it came to be that I started to translate my motifs into paper silhouettes, buildings, and stories.

There is something liberating when you work three-dimensionally.

The possibilities are endless, and most of the time the desire and the ideas are as well. It probably has a lot to do with variety in the work—everything from idea, measuring, and constructing, to the step of having the characters and environments come to life. It is a magical feeling to me that all this can happen during one day in front of me, on my desk, by using one single sheet of paper.

Fideli Sundqvist

basic materials

All you need to get going are a scalpel, a cutting mat, and paper. With just these things you can make silhouettes, images, and 3-D constructions. In time you will surely come up with several of your own ideas for how to get shapes and effects, but here are a few tips regarding tools and materials that I think are good to use when I work.

Double-sided tape
Most of the time I use double-sided tape when I assemble my paper objects. They come in in a couple of different widths. I usually use ¼" (6 mm) and ½" (12 mm).

Paper tape
I use paper tape almost daily: for sketch mounting, holding the paper sheet on the cutting mat, and for hanging images on the wall. The tape neither damages nor makes imprints on the paper.

Bone folder
A bone folder is good to have when you are folding paper and creating tabs for assembly. The edge is sharp and neat. You may also use the backside of a kitchen knife, but then you should be sure that you do not push it too hard since that may damage the paper.

Scalpel
It is sufficient to have a really good steel scalpel and several scalpel blades. My favorite blade is called 11E and is thin and pointed. It works well for cutting out both details and thicker cardboard.

Awl
An awl is good to have when you want to make holes in the paper. It is also possible to use a sewing needle, but since the awl has a handle you can easily push it through several sheets simultaneously. In addition, it is a very nice thing to have in your toolbox.

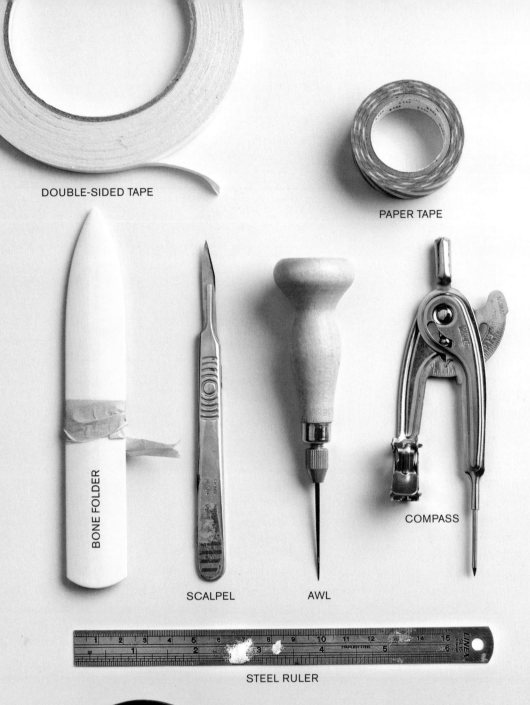

DOUBLE-SIDED TAPE

PAPER TAPE

BONE FOLDER

SCALPEL

AWL

COMPASS

STEEL RULER

CUTTING MAT

SCISSORS

Cutting mat

This transparent mat is my favorite and it has a fantastic surface. It is self-healing, light in color (does not take much attention away from the paper objects), and does not make the scalpel blade blunt quickly. It doesn't matter very much what size you use. You can do quite a lot on a small mat.

Wax paper

Wax paper or similar transparent paperlike architect film is very good to use when you are tracing templates for your projects. They are also so thin that there should not be any great difference when you cut through the sheets.

Other tools that may come in handy

- Mechanical pencil or lead pencil
- Eraser
- Brush with a round handle (to shape the paper with)
- Rx-adhesive or other universal adhesive that dries quickly
- Needle and thread (for hanging or assembly)

Compass

This comes in handy when you are creating round forms.

Steel ruler

This small ruler is one of the tools that I use most often. It is easy to use and it stays totally straight since it is made of steel. It may be handy to have a longer ruler as well when you want to trim larger sheets.

Scissors

These are ideal for cutting out a piece of paper, cutting a thread, or cutting round shapes and simple silhouettes.

PAPER

I often use regular white printer paper of about 80 grams (20 or 21 lb.) to draw on, but also to sketch my construction. Before I make the finished objects I sometimes make different sizes, forms, and compositions on the white paper in order to get a sense of how it will look. When I have completed the forms it is also simpler to choose what colors the objects should be. Through the years I have collected different kinds of paper that I like.

Most of the time, the color is the determining factor. When I first started making paper silhouettes, I mostly used somewhat higher surface weights because the silhouette broke so easily when the paper was thin. Nowadays I mostly like to work with size A4 sheets of different colors, about 27–53lb (100–200 grams). You will have to try it your own way until you find what you like. The advantage with the somewhat thinner sheets is that your hand does not get as tired and the cutting lines are finer.

I often also use some kind of cardboard in my constructions. I do that mainly in order to stabilize the paper objects. White foamboard, 3/32" (3 mm) and 3/16" (5 mm) is the most useful. It is easy to cut into and it weighs next to nothing, as opposed to regular cardboard.

GLOSSARY

Creasing

You can create a scallop or crease in the paper by using a rounded blade edge, for example, a bone folder. Creasing makes it easier to fold the paper without it being damaged and cracked. In addition, you will have the exact folds in the places you want.

Bulk

Papers that have a low weight may be thick if they have a high bulk. Some paper may be airier and therefore feel thicker if you hold it between your fingers than paper that has a higher weight. Pocket books, for instance, have a rather brittle and airy paper, but at the same time they do not weigh very much. It is simply a paper with higher bulk, but at the same time with a rather low gram weight.

Direction of the fiber

When the paper is manufactured, the cellulose fibers end up in the direction of the paper path. That way, the paper becomes more flexible in one direction. If you bend a paper carefully between your hands, you can feel a certain difference between the different directions. In thicker paper this will be more obvious. If you are going to glue two pieces of paper together, it is important to ensure that the direction of the fiber is aligned so that the paper does not bend. Since I almost exclusively work with double-sided tape, my paper constructions are not affected by this.

Gram weight/surface weight

The gram weight tells us how much the paper weighs per square meter. In a way, it also tells us a little about the thickness of the paper, but it can be misleading due to the bulk of the paper. Even though you are looking into a paper of the same name (most papers have a name) or quality, the paper will be thicker the higher the gram weight it has.

Foamboard

Foamboard may have many different names. It is also called cell carton board or centafoam panneau. What is typical for foamboard is that it is very light and stiff. It consists of polystyrene (looks like hard foam) with paper on both sides. Foamboard is very good to have when stabilizing construction, both as a foundation or to mount behind. It is also popular in modeling.

Sketching

I usually say that I am sketching when I perform the first 3-D tests. I usually use a thinner white paper, often regular printer paper (about 80 grams [20-21 lb.]), to find the forms and sizes I am looking for and also to test different compositions. This step is often open to ideas and solutions that are hard to develop when I am sitting and thinking or drawing and sketching in my notebook.

basic
techniques

Measuring and sketching

I typically use the point of the scalpel when I measure and mark where I am going to cut. In that way there will be no marks and you don't need to erase either, which may damage the paper.

Cut and snip

For details that are to be cut out and for finer silhouette cuts, I always use a scalpel. Scissors are practical when you want to quickly trim a piece of paper or cut simple figures and round shapes.

Crease

There are different tricks for how to make good-looking and sharp folds. If you have a bone folder, then you can make nice folds that are easy on the paper. By pulling the pointed part of the bone folder against a ruler you will get straight lines in the paper that are then simple to fold. Remember that the side that is upward, the one that you pull the bone folder on, is the side that will be the outside of the fold.

I prefer to turn the scalpel upside down so that the blunt edge of the scalpel creates the line. It is a matter of practicing so that you get a feeling for not cutting through the paper, since the thin blade is rather sharp even on the back edge. The benefit of the blade is that the lines become very thin and the folds become exact to the millimeter.

Test this on a different piece of paper and see how firmly or gently you must pull in order to get fine folds.

Fasten and assemble

Most often I make paper objects that will be photographed, and so I do not need to think about how they will change with time. That is why I use double-sided tape when I assemble my objects. It is easy to use and provides neat edges. However, the tape has a way of drying out and losing its adhesiveness. So if you want to be sure that an object will last, you should use glue. It is more finicky, but it lasts longer. In order to avoid fingerprints and residual glue, it is a good idea to use a brush to apply the glue where the assembly is to be made. Then you must remember to wait for the glue to dry before you go to the next step of the assembly.

silhouettes

Silhouettes are 2-D shapes and images. The easiest thing is often to cut them out with a scalpel. With larger shapes, it may work to cut them out with scissors.

Before I started with paper I worked a fair amount with graphics. It was when I was working on a series of linoleum cuts that I really discovered how amazing it is to work with my hands. Linoleum reminds me of silhouette cutting in both expression and technique.

The first images I made of paper were silhouettes. I traced my illustrations on regular printer paper and put them on top of colored sheets. Then I cut out the lines and the shapes until I could lift off the paper with the sketch and carefully pick away the shapes in between, as the image emerged.

Remember that all lines must be kept together when making a silhouete. In a face, the eyes, nose, and mouth must be attached to the facial contour or to each other (where at least one part should be attached to the facial contour). For this reason, no objects can be loose. This will affect the expression of the image and it may take a while before you find a way to do it that you like. The silhouette is formed by the paper that is kept, as much as by what is cut away.

One of the finest details is the shadow play that arises behind the paper cut. You can enhance the shadow by mounting a small spacer behind the cut. You can also test different kinds of lighting. In addition to the automatic play of light behind the image, I often draw shadows to produce more depth to the image.

Linoleum cut

A detailed silhouette where each thin line keeps the image together.

SILHOUETTE CUTS

Cut out the shapes, figures, or letters and mount on a stick and place in a potted plant. Or let the figures become actors in a story. Feel free to create an environment where the figures can act as well, such as a theater.

TOOLS	Silhouettes step by step
PAPER	1. Trace the template or make your own shapes and figures on a piece of wax paper.
PENCIL	
PAPER TAPE	2. Place the template on the paper you want to use for the figure. It is a good idea to use paper that is a bit thicker, about 150–200 grams (5.3–7.0 ozs.).
SCISSORS	
SCALPEL	
CUTTING MAT	

Silhouettes step by step

1. Trace the template or make your own shapes and figures on a piece of wax paper.
2. Place the template on the paper you want to use for the figure. It is a good idea to use paper that is a bit thicker, about 150–200 grams (5.3–7.0 ozs.).
Fasten the wax paper with tape so that the paper doesn't slide. It is best to use paper tape.
3. Cut with a scalpel along the already drawn lines.
4. Fasten the silhouette with a piece of tape to the top of a stick, in a mobile hanger, or to what you think is most suitable.
It may be nice to pull a thread through and hang the silhouette in a window or on a nail against a wall.

TOOLS	Silhouettes step by step
PAPER	
PENCIL	
SPACER TAPE	
PAPER TAPE	
SCISSORS	
SCALPEL	
CUTTING MAT	

Silhouettes step by step

1. Make a drawing with connected shapes (all parts must be connected). Pay attention to the fact that what is left after you have made the cuts must be continuous. It may be a little tricky to think correctly about it the first time, but after you have practiced it will become clearer. Use printer paper of about 80 grams (20-21 lb.). Consider that the more detailed an image is, the more brittle and more difficult it will be to have nice lines.
2. Place the sketching paper on the selected piece of paper and fasten with tape so that it doesn't slide. It is best if you use paper tape.
3. Cut out the parts that will be removed (the white ones on the image) with a scalpel.

Shadow theater with silhouettes mounted on sticks.

geometric figures

All the steps are included here—sketch, measure, cut, crease, and assemble—in order to achieve a 3-D object. The figures work both as sculptures and as a foundation for building up several different-looking objects and environments.

It is hard to create round shapes in paper, but you can do so by using geometric shapes to achieve round spheres. Later in the book, I will also review other methods.

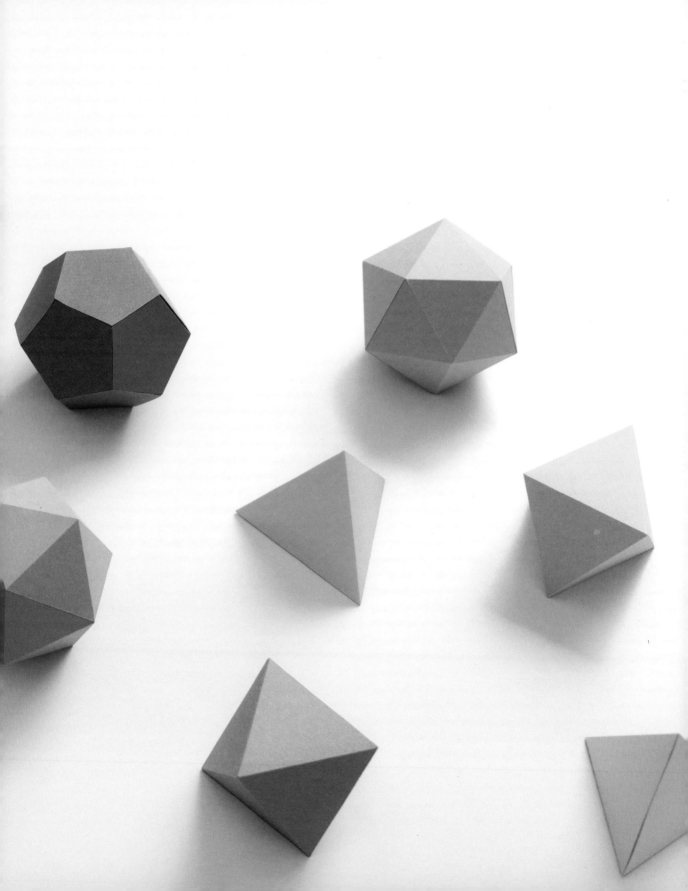

GEOMETRIC FIGURES

The first three platonic bodies are quick to learn. It may be a bit tricky to fasten the last side. The last two, the dodecahedron and the icosahedron, are a bit demanding timewise when it comes to measuring and cutting out, but they are folded based on the same principle as the others. Fasten one side at a time until the shape is closed and you have a geometric figure.

1. Trace the template on wax paper.
2. Place the wax paper on the selected paper. Fasten with tape, preferably paper tape, so that the paper does not slide.
3. Use a scalpel and cut out the figure along the outer edges.
4. Remove the wax paper. Place the ruler along the dashed lines (see template) and pull with the bone folder.
5. Crease all edges.
6. Mount by fastening the double-sided tape or put glue on the folded tabs. Let dry, if you are using glue.

PAPER
PENCIL
DOUBLE-SIDED TAPE OR GLUE
ANY BONE FOLDER
PAPER TAPE
SCALPEL
WAX PAPER
STEEL RULER

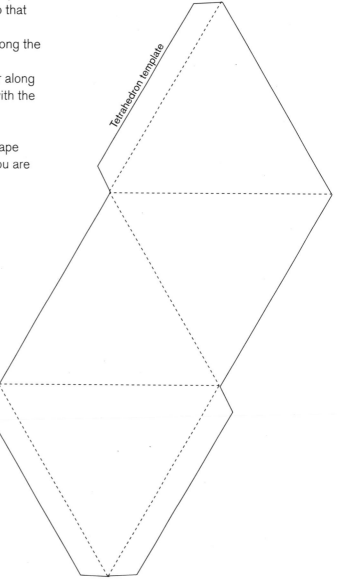

Tetrahedron template

TETRAHEDRON
1. The cut-out template.
2. Template showing creased lines.
3. The template with double-sided tape on the tabs.
4. The finished tetrahedron.

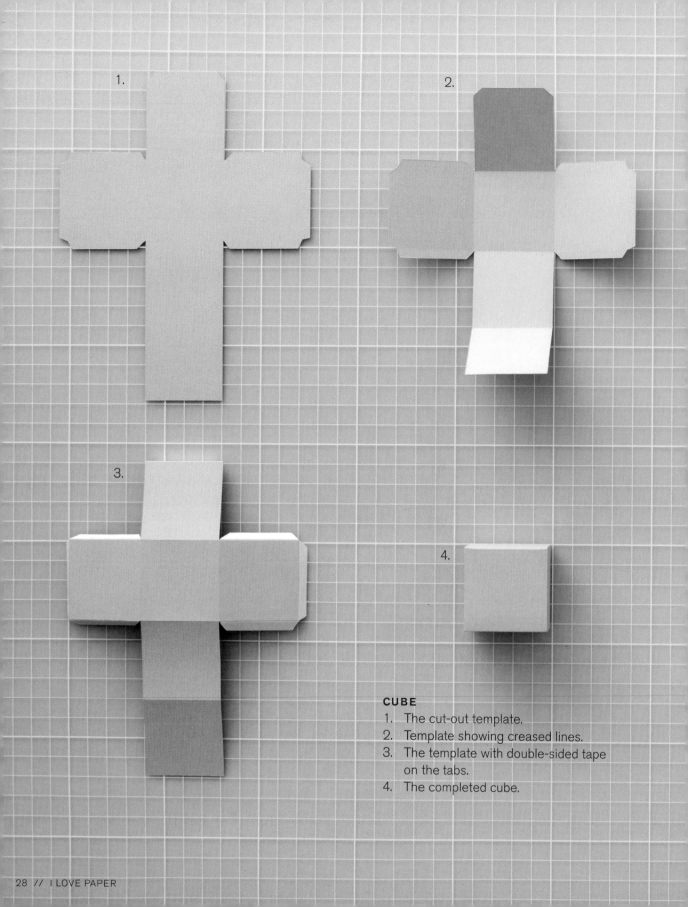

CUBE

1. The cut-out template.
2. Template showing creased lines.
3. The template with double-sided tape on the tabs.
4. The completed cube.

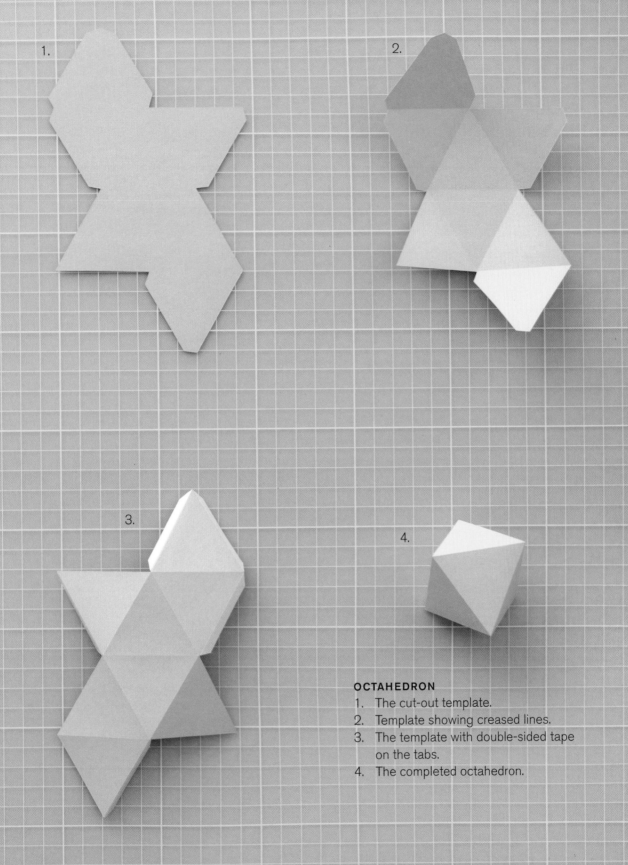

OCTAHEDRON

1. The cut-out template.
2. Template showing creased lines.
3. The template with double-sided tape on the tabs.
4. The completed octahedron.

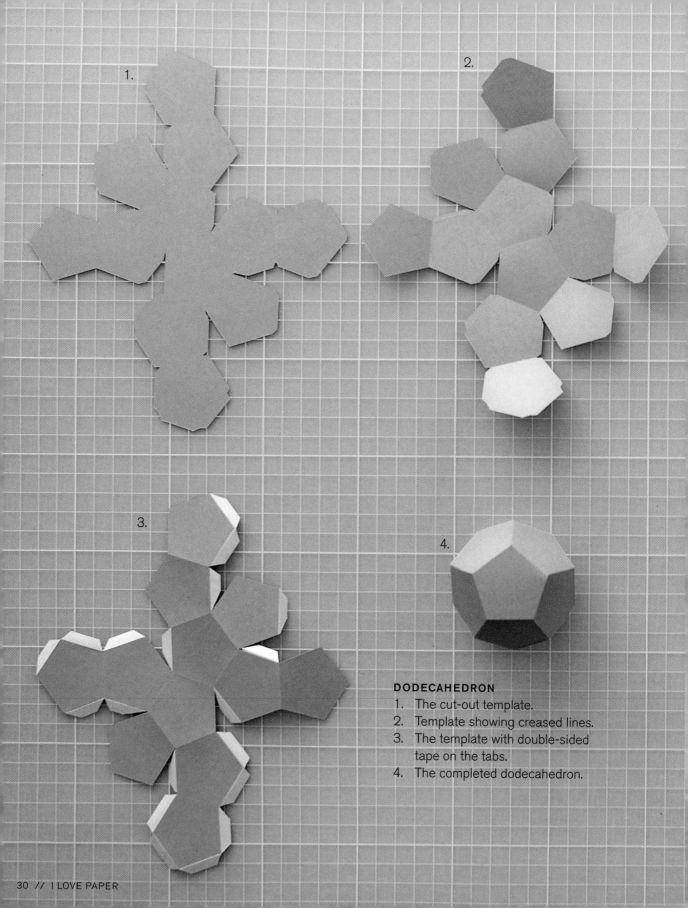

DODECAHEDRON

1. The cut-out template.
2. Template showing creased lines.
3. The template with double-sided tape on the tabs.
4. The completed dodecahedron.

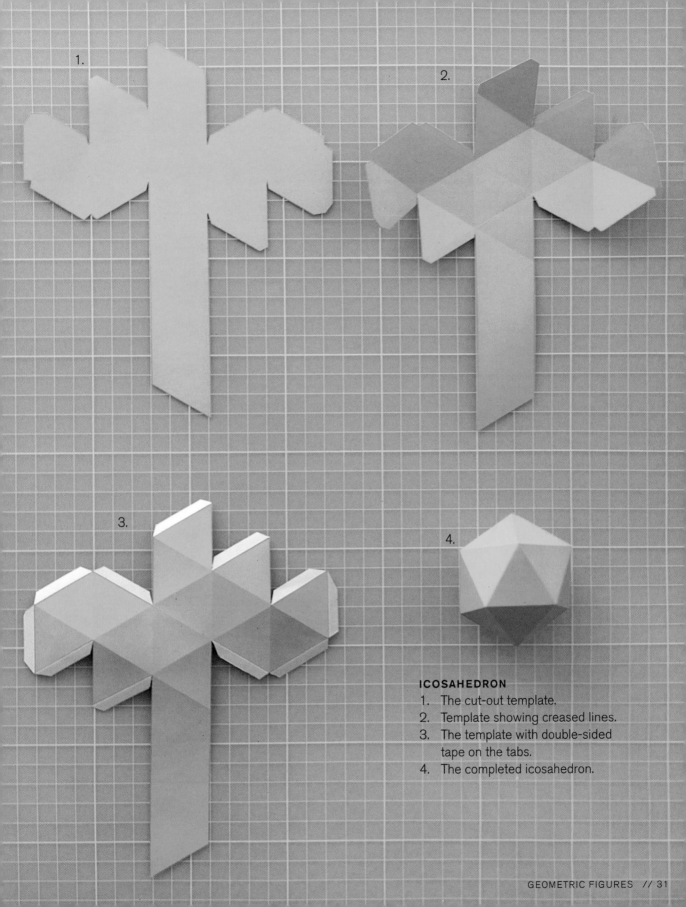

1.

2.

3.

4.

ICOSAHEDRON

1. The cut-out template.
2. Template showing creased lines.
3. The template with double-sided tape on the tabs.
4. The completed icosahedron.

Octahedron template: refer to the description on page 29.

Icosahedron template: refer to the description on page 31.

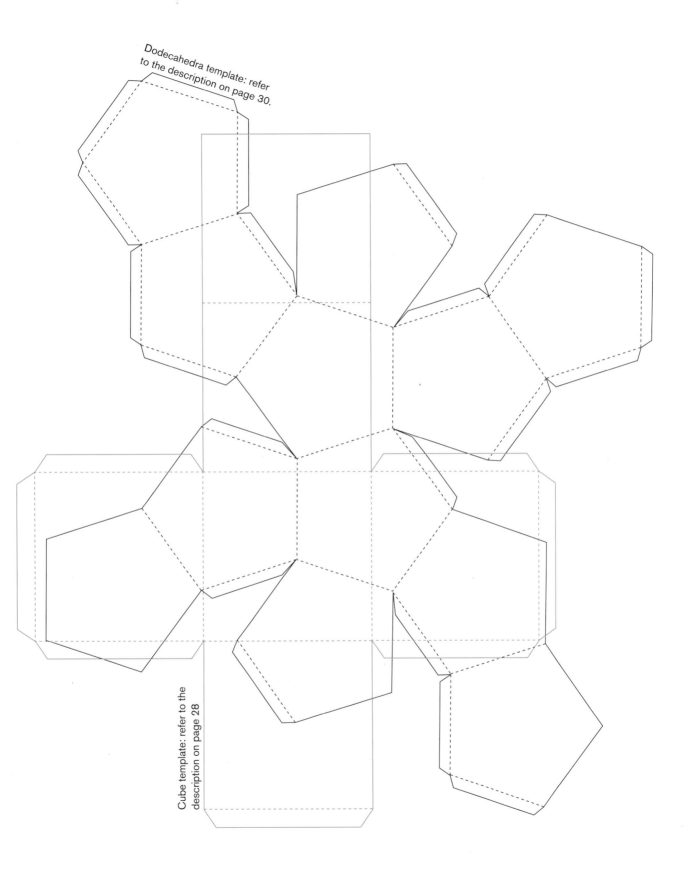

Dodecahedra template: refer to the description on page 30.

Cube template: refer to the description on page 28

food

Some of my favorite themes to base my work on are food, fruit, and coffee time. It is fun to create realistic-looking paper objects and to try to find ways to achieve details that are as effective as possible—such as the rounding of the egg yolk and its shine or the wrinkly texture of the arugula leaves.

I usually look at real objects, both before and during the course of the work. From these objects you can then create images that are impossible to stage in real life, but totally possible in the world of paper.

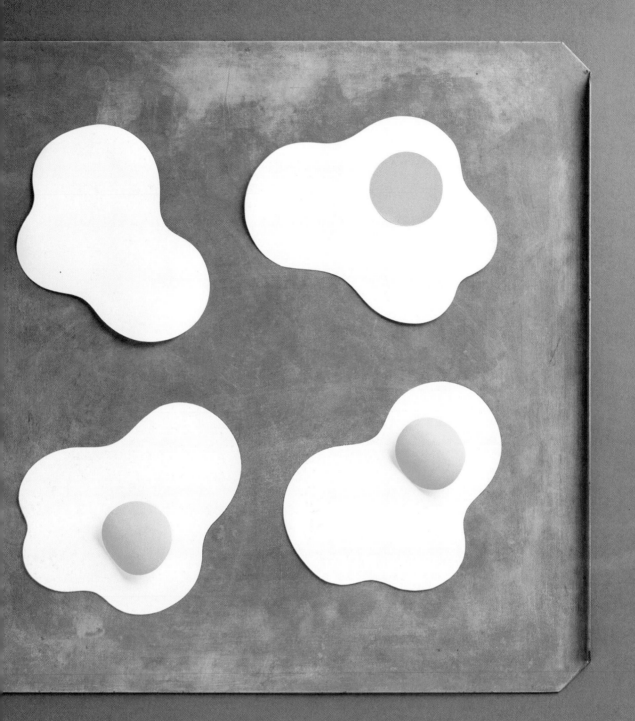

Bacon template

Egg template

Arugula template

EGGS

Fried eggs in paper are among the simplest things you can make. I am very enchanted myself with the paper egg. When it is illuminated and photographed it will have a 3-D effect in all its simplicity.

TOOLS
PAPER
PENCIL
DOUBLE-SIDED TAPE OR GLUE
SPACER TAPE
PAPER TAPE
BRUSH
SCALPEL
STEEL RULER

Eggs step by step

1. Trace the egg template on wax paper.
2. Place the template on the selected paper. Fasten the wax paper with tape so that the paper does not slide. It is best if you use paper tape. Cut out with a scalpel.
3. Pull with the brush handle along the back of the egg yolk so that it gets a slightly rounded shape.
4. Fasten the egg and the yolk with a bit of spacer tape to obtain a 3-D aspect.

Arugula step by step

1. Trace the template for the arugula leaf on wax paper.
2. Place the template on the selected paper. Fasten the wax paper with tape so that the paper does not slide. It is best if you use paper tape. Cut out with a scalpel.
3. Place the ruler in the middle of the blade and pull with the bone folder. Crease the leaf.
4. Put the leaf over the brush handle and press it together carefully so that it appears wrinkled.

BACON

Bacon is simple to make. The wavy form creates an illusion and provides dimension. I think the choice of color is important to bring out the special characteristics of bacon.

TOOLS
PAPER
PENCIL
SPACER TAPE
PAPER TAPE
BRUSH
SCALPEL
CUTTING MAT
WAX PAPER

Bacon step by step

1. Place a pink sheet (size A4) of paper lengthwise on the cutting mat. Cut strips that have a width of 1.2 – 1.6" (3–4 cm).
2. Put double-sided tape on a white sheet A4 of paper in landscape mode so that it covers about 2.4" (6 cm) of the sheet.
3. Turn the paper over and cut a few different wavy lines. Be sure that you cut on the side of the sheet that has double-sided tape on the back.
4. Remove the protective tape and fasten the white wavy strips on the pink ones, varying the spaces between them. If the white strips stick out, you just need to make clean cuts along the shape of the pink strip.
5. Add shape to the strips with the aid of a brush by pulling the handle along the bacon slices in a few different places on both the front and the back until you feel that you have nice piece of wavy bacon.

One of the first projects I made after graduation was a
series of images that consisted of a three-dish menu.

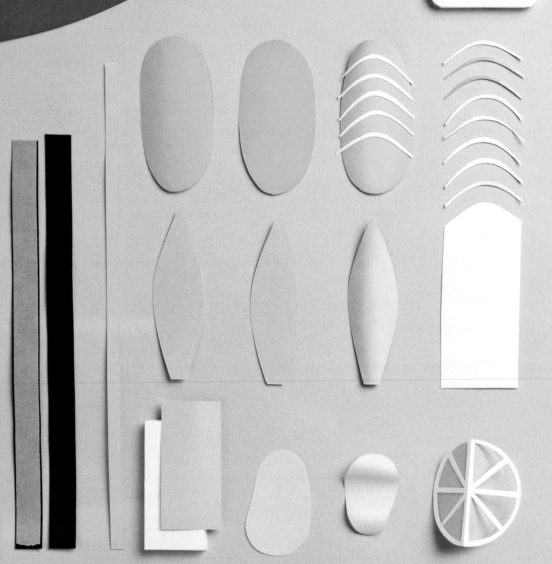

TOOLS
PAPER
PENCIL
SPACER TAPE
DOUBLE-SIDED TAPE OR GLUE
FOAM BOARD $\frac{3}{16}$" (5MM)
PAPER TAPE
SCALPEL
WAX PAPER
STEEL RULER

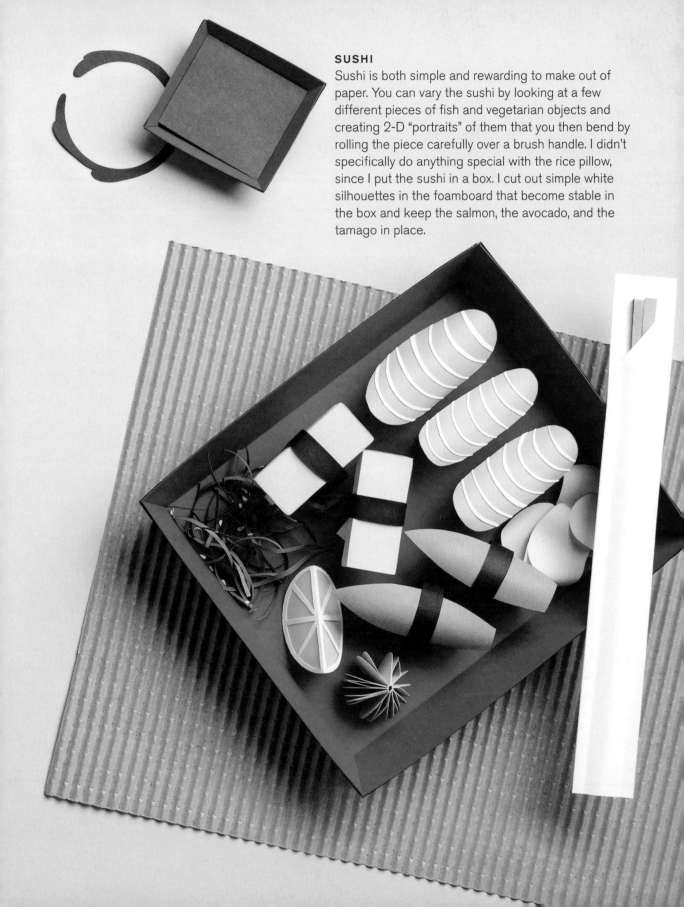

SUSHI

Sushi is both simple and rewarding to make out of paper. You can vary the sushi by looking at a few different pieces of fish and vegetarian objects and creating 2-D "portraits" of them that you then bend by rolling the piece carefully over a brush handle. I didn't specifically do anything special with the rice pillow, since I put the sushi in a box. I cut out simple white silhouettes in the foamboard that become stable in the box and keep the salmon, the avocado, and the tamago in place.

Sushi step by step

1. Trace the rice template on wax paper. Make a template for each piece of sushi that you want.
2. Put the templates on the white foamboard. Fasten the wax paper with tape so that the paper does not slide. It is best if you use paper tape. Cut out with a scalpel.
3. Fasten double-sided tape on black paper and cut strips that are about 0.4" (1 cm) wide.
4. Trace the templates for salmon, avocado, and tamago on the wax paper and place them on suitable colors and cut out the shapes.
5. For the salmon, it is a good idea to make white lines so that you get a true salmon feeling. You can achieve this by fastening double-sided tape on the back of white paper and then cut out rounded lines (similar to the bacon, on page 39) that you fasten on the pink shape. If the white lines stick out, it is easy to do a clean cut or cut away the pieces. After that, fasten the salmon by using a piece of the double-sided tape on one of the sushi pieces.
6. By pulling the brush along the back of the avocado you can get a rounded shape that most resembles an avocado "character." Fasten the avocado on one of the rice pillows by assembling a piece of spacer tape or double-sided tape between the avocado and the edge of the rice pillow.
7. You can also apply a piece of double-sided tape on the lower edge of each rice pillow, so that they stand up on the table.
8. For the tamago it is good if you mount the light yellow paper shape on a piece of foamboard, because then the tamago itself will be a bit thicker. In order to cover the edges of the foamboard you can cut out a strip of the yellow paper that is $3/16$" (5 mm) wide. Fasten the circle cut-out by first putting the double-sided tape around the edge of the foamboard.
9. Fasten the tamago on one of the sushi pieces by attaching a piece of double-sided tape between the tamago and the rice pillow.
10. Loosen the protective plastic on the back of the black strip and wrap the strip around the rice pillow and the avocado. Start on the bottom of the sushi piece and make the strip run around the entire piece before you cut it. Do the same thing with the tamago piece.

Lemon step by step

1. Trace the templates for the lemon on wax paper.
2. Place the templates on the selected pieces of paper. Fasten the wax paper with tape so that the paper doesn't slide. It is best if you use paper tape. Cut it out with a scalpel.
3. Place the ruler on the dashed lines (see template) and pull the bone folder along it. Do the same thing with the white part that creates the details of the lemon.
4. Put the white shape on top of the yellow one and fasten small pieces of double-sided tape in at least two spots so that it stays in place.
5. If you want, you can cut out a few seeds and mount them in the yellow wedges.

Ginger step by step

1. Use the scalpel and cut out a few uneven rounded shapes in light yellow paper.
2. Use the brush handle to bend the ginger on both sides so that it will get a wavy shape.
3. Make a few pieces and place them next to the sushi.

Sea grass step by step

1. Take a green piece of paper and cut thin strips of $5/64–1/8$" (2–3 mm).
2. Use the brush handle to bend the strips on both sides so that they get a wavy shape.
3. Cut off the strips and roll them up carefully into little balls between your hands.
4. Place the sea grass balls next to the sushi pieces.
5. Cut out small sesame seeds on your chosen paper that can be scattered when everything is in place.

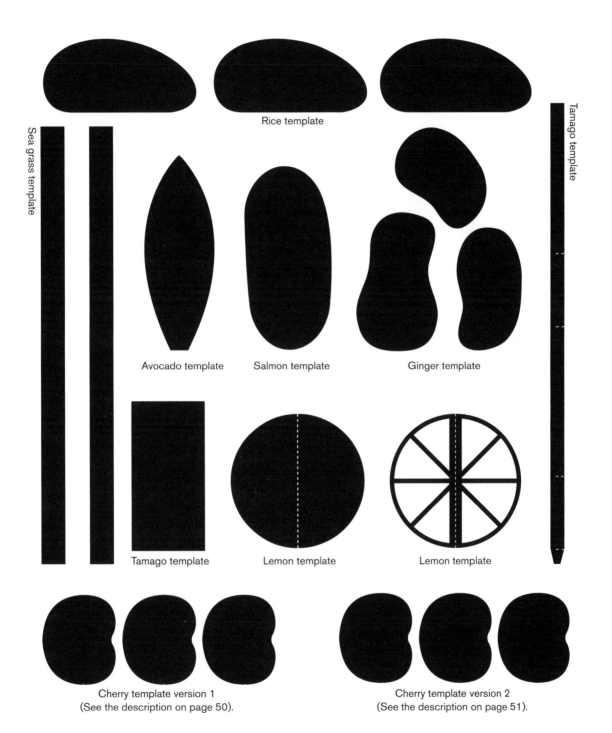

Rice template

Tamago template

Sea grass template

Avocado template

Salmon template

Ginger template

Tamago template

Lemon template

Lemon template

Cherry template version 1
(See the description on page 50).

Cherry template version 2
(See the description on page 51).

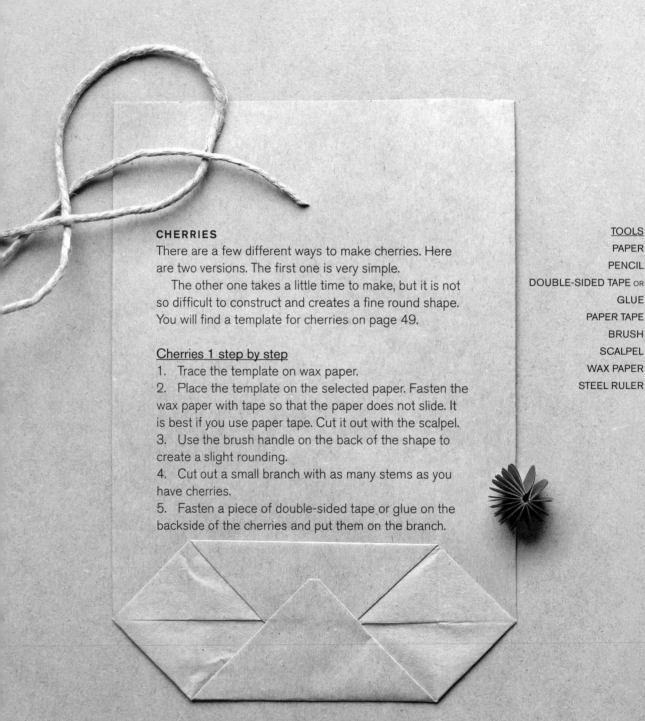

CHERRIES

There are a few different ways to make cherries. Here are two versions. The first one is very simple.

The other one takes a little time to make, but it is not so difficult to construct and creates a fine round shape. You will find a template for cherries on page 49.

<u>Cherries 1 step by step</u>
1. Trace the template on wax paper.
2. Place the template on the selected paper. Fasten the wax paper with tape so that the paper does not slide. It is best if you use paper tape. Cut it out with the scalpel.
3. Use the brush handle on the back of the shape to create a slight rounding.
4. Cut out a small branch with as many stems as you have cherries.
5. Fasten a piece of double-sided tape or glue on the backside of the cherries and put them on the branch.

<u>TOOLS</u>
PAPER
PENCIL
DOUBLE-SIDED TAPE OR
GLUE
PAPER TAPE
BRUSH
SCALPEL
WAX PAPER
STEEL RULER

Cherries 2 step by step

1. Trace the template on a wax paper.
2. Place the template on the selected paper. Fasten the wax paper with tape so that the paper does not slide. It is best if you use paper tape. Cut out about 10 cherries with a scalpel.
3. Place the ruler on the dashed line (see template on page 49) and pull the bone folder along it. Crease all cherries.
4. Fasten the double-sided tape in the middle of the cherry half (on the exterior of the creased edge).
5. Mount all the pieces until the last piece is fastened to the first one. Repeat this until you have as many cherries as you wish.
6. Cut out a small branch with as many stems as you have cherries.
7. Fasten a piece of double-sided tape on the tip of each branch and attach one cherry at a time.

APPLE
Making an apple very much resembles making Cherry 2 – the only difference is the shape. With the apple you can create variations such as apple wedges or apple halves, where the core can become a third dimension.

Systembolaget's (the State Liquor Store's)
gift cartons/bags, fall 2013

TOOLS

PAPER

PENCIL

SPACER TAPE

DOUBLE-SIDED TAPE OR GLUE

BONE FOLDER

PAPER TAPE

SCALPEL

WAX PAPER

STEEL RULER

TIPS!

If you want to make fall leaves, just mix different
colors. You can also wrinkle the shape after you
have cut it out to give it further character.

Apple step by step

1. Trace the template on wax paper.
2. Place the template on the selected paper. Fasten the wax paper with tape so that the paper doesn't slide. It is best if you use paper tape. Cut out about 10 apples with a scalpel.
3. Place the ruler on the dashed line (see template to the right) and pull along it with the bone folder. Crease all apple parts.
4. Fasten the double-sided tape in the middle of the apples. It is sufficient to fasten it on half of the templates (on the outside of the creased edge).
5. Mount all the pieces until the last piece is connected to the first one.
6. On dark brown paper, fasten double-sided tape about ³⁄₁₆" (5 mm) from the edge of the sheet.
7. Clip out or cut small strips.
8. Roll up until you have used about 3" (8 cm) of the strip.
9. Wrap around a bit of double-sided tape at the top of the "apple beard" and attach to the apple. Spread out the brown leaves of the strip.
10. Cut out a piece of stem from the brown paper and attach it to the top of the apple.
11. If you want, you can also cut out a leaf and mount it next to the stem.

Apple wedge step by step

1–4. See above, the same as Apple step by step.
5. Assemble the pieces, but do not fasten the first and last piece.
6. Cut out an apple template that will not be creased.
7. Cut out two drop shapes which will be the apple core. Fasten two pieces of spacer tape on the back and assemble on a piece of paper that covers the holes.
8. Fasten double-sided tape on the back and then assemble the first and last piece of the apple accordion.
9. Cut out two brown seeds that you can attach with glue in the core.
10. Just as with the entire apple it is a nice idea to assemble a small branch with a leaf and a little bit of "apple beard" at the bottom.

Apple template

Apple beard template

Tasteless

I created these images in cooperation with Olivia Jeczmyk and Joanna Lavén for Restaurang 1900. At the same time, I was attending an art history evening class at Stockholm University and I became very fascinated by the symbolism found in the still lifes from the seventeenth century.

It was fun to let the paper attain a darker and heavier ambiance, because usually it has an energetic, playful, and colorful feeling. In addition, I have always been amused by trompe l'oeil images.

flowers and leaves

It is possible to create both realistic-looking and more graphical flowers. In this example, I would like to show you how to create a daisy. Since the petals are rather thin and long, it is a bit brittle to work with.

It may therefore be a good idea to remember not to cut the petals too close to the middle of the flower. You will find the template on page 63.

TOOLS
PAPER
FLOWER TAPE
PENCIL
DOUBLE-SIDED TAPE or
GLUE
PAPER TAPE
SCALPEL
WAX PAPER
STEEL RULER
STEEL PIN

Daisy step by step

1. Trace the template on wax paper.
2. Place the template on the white paper. Fasten the wax paper with tape so that the paper does not slide. It is best if you use paper tape.
3. Cut out the contour of the flower with a scalpel.
4. Make two identical flowers so that there are twice as many petals on the daisy.
5. On a piece of yellow paper, fasten a double-sided tape about 3/16" (5 mm) from the edge of the paper and then cut out the strip on the other side of the tape.
6. Clip or cut out tiny little strips like bangs.
7. Place the two white flowers on top of each other, but with a small rotation so that the petals do not lie exactly on top of each other. Then cut two x's in the middle of the flower.
8. Loosen the protective plastic from the tape on the yellow strip and roll up until you have used about 3" (8 cm) of the strip, then cut it off.
9. Fold down the tabs in the middle of the flower and place the yellow rolled-up strip in the middle.
10. Fold out the outermost layers of the yellow strips so that they are nicely spread out. You can also roll the white petals lightly with the help of a brush handle so that their shape becomes more alive.
11. Press one steel pin in about 3/16" (5 mm) on the bottom in the middle of the yellow. The pin stays in place quite well with the help of the double-sided tape on the yellow strip.
12. Wind flower tape around the wire stem, the under side of the flower, and the white tabs that surround the yellow middle. Pull a few turns tightly before you wind the tape downwards on the stem until it is covered.

The inspiration for the flower map came from old-fashioned school posters.

Daisy template, petals.
Refer to description on
page 60.

Template for the middle of the daisy

Leaf templates

Leaves step by step

1. Trace the template on wax paper.
2. Place the template on the selected paper. Fasten the wax paper with tape so that the paper does not slide. It is best if you use paper tape. Cut out with a scalpel.
3. Place the ruler in the middle of the leaf (along the dashed line) and pull with the bone folder.
4. Pull with the brush handle along the back of the leaf so that it gets a slightly rounded shape.

Flowers made of paper

It is a very rewarding feeling to make flowers out of paper. The thin and fragile parts that are features of real flowers are related to what is in the structure of the paper. It is a very good idea to use thin sheets for the flower petals, since they are so flexible and therefore easily resemble real flowers. It may be a good idea to test other types of paper as well, such as here where I have made the flowers out of newspaper.

masquerade

These resemble silhouette cutouts. These also work well when mounted on a stick and used to accentuate a costume at a party or used as a mustache decoration on a flower pot.

FEATHERS

The feathers may be used in different ways in your hair or you can fasten them on a rubber band and make a Native American headpiece. They are also beautiful as decoration.

Spectacles template

Mustache template

Pipe template

Feather template

TOOLS
PAPER
STICKS
PENCIL
DOUBLE-SIDED TAPE OR
GLUE
BONE FOLDER
PAPER TAPE
SCISSORS
SCALPEL
WAX PAPER
STEEL RULER

Spectacles, mustache, and pipe step by step

1. Trace the templates on wax paper.
2. Place the templates on the selected paper, preferably a bit thicker at around 150–200 grams (40–53 lb).
Fasten the wax paper with tape so that the paper does not slide. It is best if you use paper tape. Cut out with a scalpel.
3. Assemble the parts of the pipe with the help of double-sided tape.
4. Attach the spectacles, mustache, and pipe at the very top of one stick each.

Feather step by step

1. Trace the template on wax paper.
2. Place the template on the chosen paper. Fasten the wax paper with tape so that the paper does not slide. It is best if you use paper tape. Cut out with a scalpel.
3. Put the ruler in the middle of the feather and draw a line with a pencil.
4. Cut thin strips in the feather on either side of the pencil line. It works just as well to use scissors as it does to use a scalpel.
5. Ensure that you stay a few millimeters from the middle, so that you do not chop off the feather when you cut or cut out strips on both sides.

Fortune-teller hat step by step >>>

1. Make a regular fortune-teller out of white paper (the fortune-teller is folded into a square).
2. When the fortune-teller is complete, measure the triangles inside and cut triangles of the same size but with different colors.
3. You can either fasten double-sided tape or put glue on the back of the triangles and mount them one after the other in the fortune-teller.

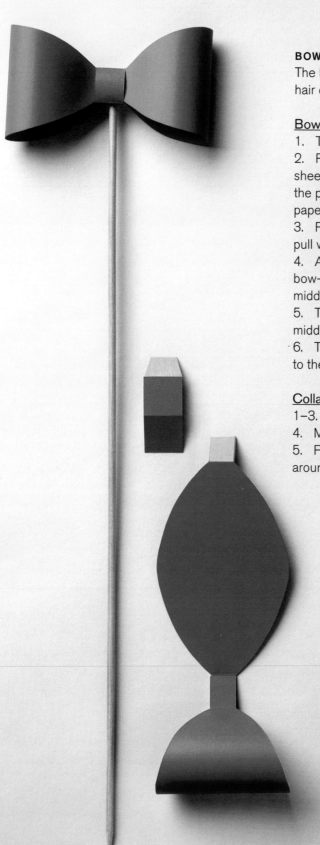

BOW TIE

The bow tie looks good both as a bow in your hair or as an accessory for a costume.

Bow tie step by step

1. Trace the templates on wax paper.
2. Place the templates on the chosen paper sheets. Fasten the wax paper with tape so that the paper does not slide. It is a good idea to use paper tape. Cut out with a scalpel.
3. Place the ruler along the dashed lines and pull with the bone folder and fold.
4. Attach double-sided tape on both tabs on the bow-tie template and attach one at a time in the middle of the bow tie.
5. Take the bow-tie knot and fold it around the middle of the bow tie.
6. Then attach the bow tie with a piece of tape to the top of the stick.

Collar step by step

1–3. See above, same as the bow tie.
4. Make a small hole on both edges of the collar.
5. Pull a ribbon through the holes and fasten around the neck by tying a bow.

COLLAR

The collar is easy to make and creates a nice play of light with all the folds. It is easy to customize both in width and neck measurements.

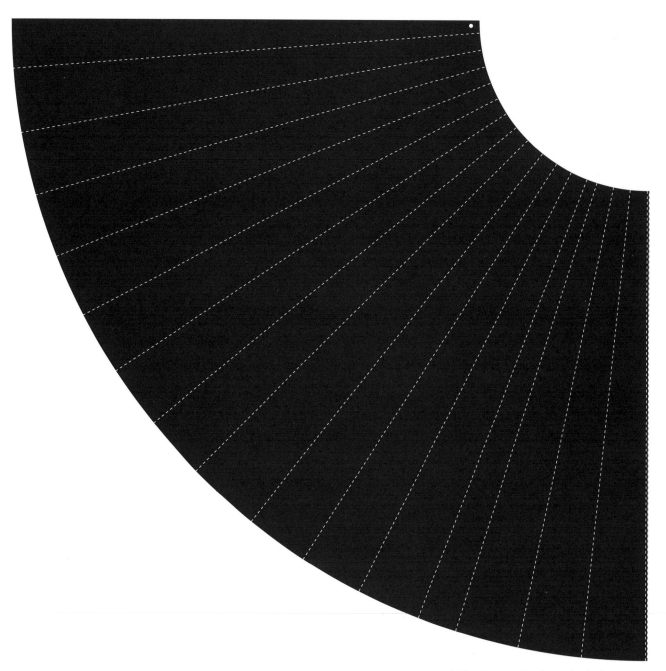

Half collar template (traced twice).
See the description on page 76.

Bow tie template. Refer to the description on page 76.

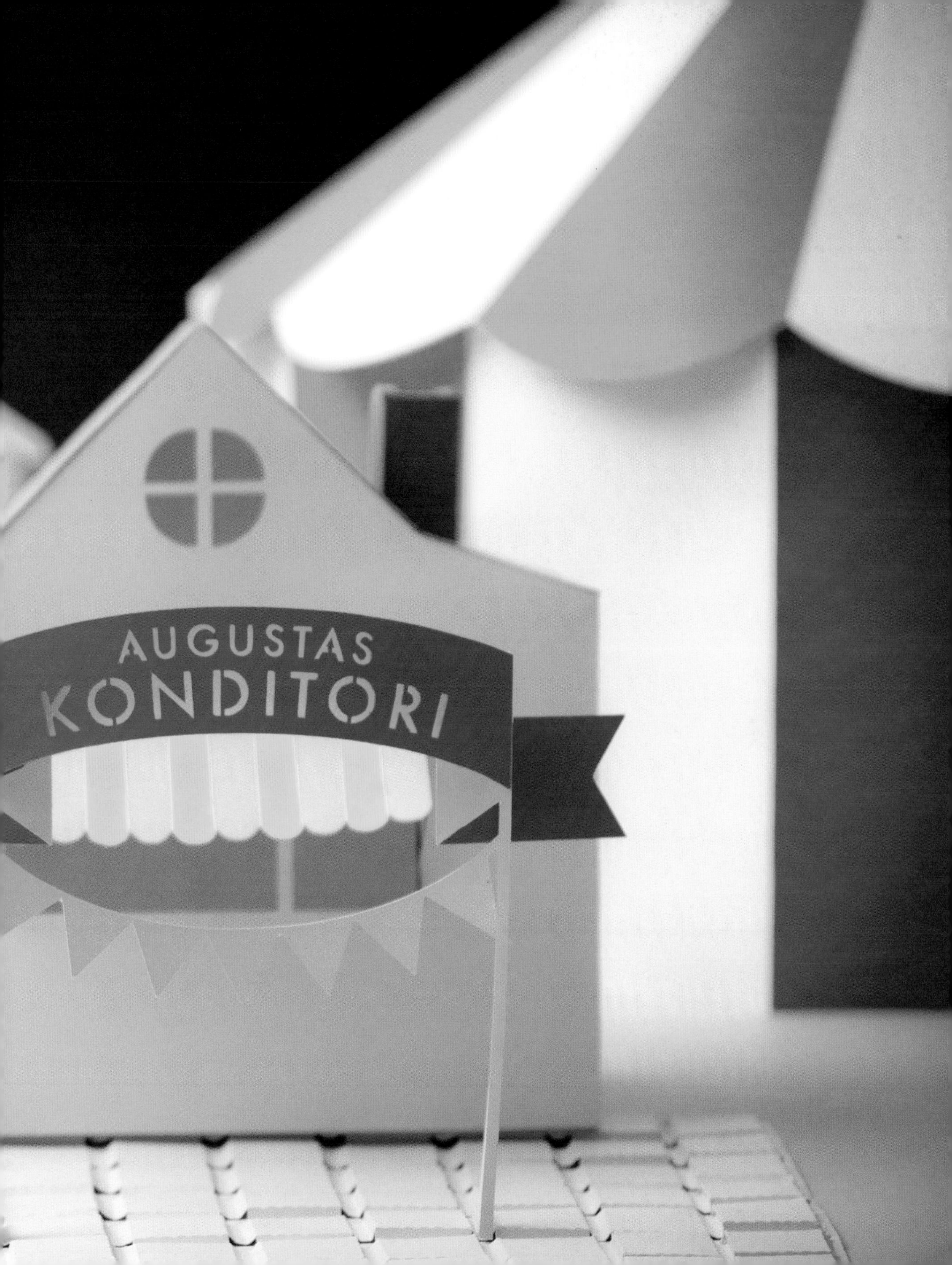
AUGUSTAS
KONDITORI

School project

The story about Tilly & Gul was written during my graduate work at University College of Arts, Crafts and Design (Konstfack). During the ten weeks that the project lasted, I had the time to test different methods of constructing, composing, lighting, and photographing that laid the groundwork for the job I have today.

It was like finding my way home when I worked with my hands, constructed objects, environments, and characters in paper of different colors. The different steps in the work process were varied in a zestful and inspiring way. In addition, objects were completed pretty quickly. When working with paper, everything is involved from idea, sketching, measuring, and constructing to arranging the objects in the existing or built up stage design.

tilly & gul

Prior to the work with Tilly and Gul, I had only completed a few 3-D constructions, so most of the paper technology was unknown to me. Sometimes I could barely see where the project would end up, but from time to time I had an image before my eyes that provided me direction on how I should continue my work.

I remember the first 3-D paper image that came into my head. It was a construction under water where the young elephant, Tilly, dove into the turquoise sea for a red spool of thread among orange corals and sea grass. The spool of thread would bring her onwards to the adventure on the little island out at sea.

To me, the image, the feeling, or the ambiance, have always come before the words. In a way, that order may feel backwards, but narration with images is more direct to me. The image or the mood creates the character and the story. In this way, the work process and the technique become very important and central to coming up with new ideas.

During the work with Tilly and Gul, I sketched on printer paper to find shapes and compositions. Many tests were required in order to succeed with the "conversion" of a 3-D object to a flat template that then would be turned into a 3-D object again. It was especially hard to create the round objects. I have further developed many of the steps for Tilly and Gul into new projects.

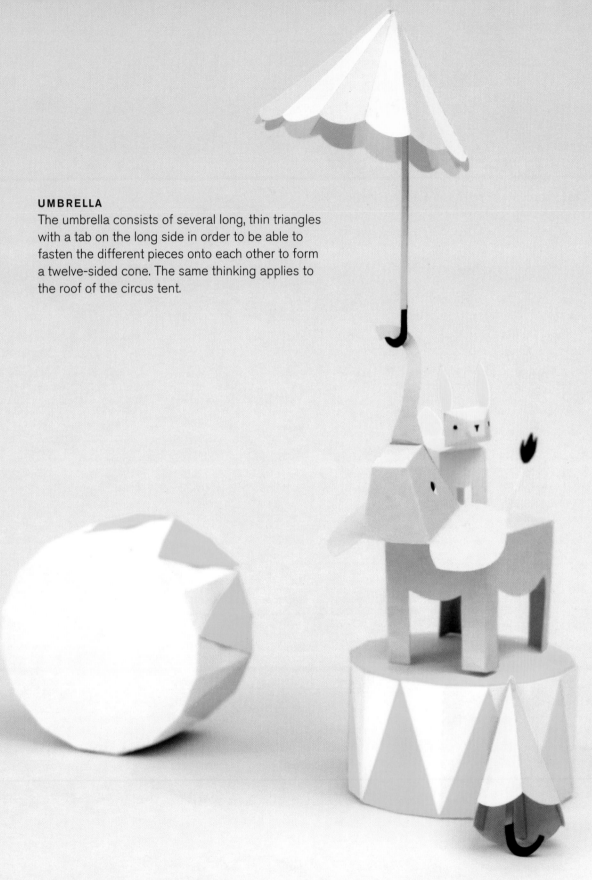

UMBRELLA

The umbrella consists of several long, thin triangles with a tab on the long side in order to be able to fasten the different pieces onto each other to form a twelve-sided cone. The same thinking applies to the roof of the circus tent.

CLOUDS

Clouds are very easy to create and it is possible to vary them in many ways. If you place two clouds on top of each other, whose "rolls" are heading in different directions, and place spacer tape between them, you will get a simple, nice, and 2-D cloud.

If you take a cloud that looks the same and pull a bone folder along the dashed lines, then you can fold the cloud rolls' shapes, every other down and every other up, and in that way you get a 3-D impression. This cloud creates a beautiful play of light due to its different angles.

Test by copying the clouds and adding lines with drops on the lower edge. These are easy to make big or small and they benefit from being presented in different colors.

TOOLS
PAPER
PENCIL
DOUBLE-SIDED TAPE
BONE FOLDER
NEEDLE AND THREAD
PAPER TAPE
SCALPEL
WAX PAPER
STEEL RULER

11. Fold down the top-most edges of the gray paper so that two tabs are formed that you can later mount inside the umbrella.

12. Take a piece of black paper and fasten a bit of double-sided tape on it.

13. Remove the protective tape and place the gray handle so that the hook is filled by the black paper.

14. Cut out the shape on the hook so that it becomes black.

15. Take another piece of black paper with double-sided tape and fasten it to the other side of the hook. Cut out the shape of the hook again so that it becomes black on both sides.

16. Remove the protective plastic on the upper-most tab of the handle and mount both the glued surfaces inside the umbrella so that the handle ends up in the middle of the inner tip of the umbrella.

You do not need to use all 16 parts when you make the umbrella. Use the amount to make the form into what you want. If, for example, you want a closed umbrella, maybe it is sufficient to have 4 mounted pieces. It is very simple to convert the umbrella into a circus tent.

Umbrella step by step

1. Trace the template 16 times on wax paper.

2. Choose two different colors of paper for the umbrella. Place 8 templates on each piece of paper. Fasten the wax paper with tape so that the paper does not slide. It is best if you use paper tape.

3. Use a scalpel and cut out the templates along the outer edges.

4. Remove the wax paper. Place the ruler along the dashed lines (see template) and pull with the bone folder. Crease all edges.

5. Apply double-sided tape or glue the folded tabs. Attach the parts to each other so that there are alternating colors until you attach the last piece to the first. Let dry between each "assembly" if you used glue.

6. Trace the umbrella handle on wax paper.

7. Use the scalpel and cut 2 strips of gray paper and mount double-sided tape on one of the strips. Wait to remove the protective plastic.

8. Place double-sided tape on the other strip as well, but let it only cover about a quarter of it.

9. Remove the protective tape on the strip that has the tape along the entire length and fasten the other strip along it so that they are glued together, including the quarter where there is still protective plastic.

10. Place the template so that the top of the handle is lying along the top-most part of the assembled gray paper (where the protective plastic remains). Cut along the dashed lines.

Circus tent step by step

1. Follow the same principle as in items 1–7 in "Umbrella step by step". In the umbrella example you use 8 parts of each color. When you make the tents, feel free to add one or two parts of each color to enlarge the tent diameter and thereby get a less pronounced tip.

2. Also trace the rectangular template in as many parts as needed for the roof.

3. Cut out the same amount of parts of each color and fasten the double-sided tape along the tabs.

4. Loosen the tape and assemble piece by piece until you close the lower part of the tent.

5. Place the tent roof on top of the lower part of the tent.

Umbrella template

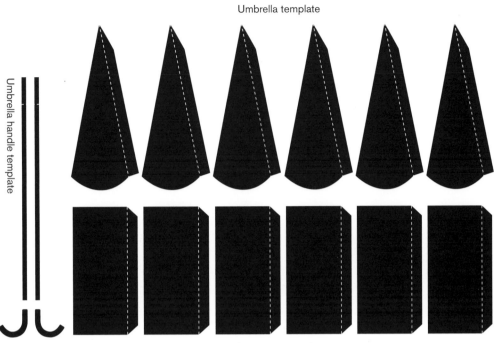

Umbrella handle template

Circus tent template

Cloud template

ELEPHANT

The first time I created an elephant in paper was for a little folding set with three animals. I tested quite a lot of shapes before I found a suitable elephant character. The elephant's square stomach enables you to create it both standing, lying, and sitting, depending on how you place the legs. In this example, I showed how you can create a lying elephant that will also have a little secret compartment in its stomach.

Elephant step by step

1. Trace the template on wax paper.
2. Place the template on the selected paper. Fasten with tape so that the paper does not slide. It is best if you use paper tape. Cut it out with a scalpel.
3. Remove the wax paper. Place the ruler along the dashed lines (see template) and pull with the bone folder.
4. Crease all edges.
5. Mount the double-sided tape or put some glue on the folded tabs and attach one page at a time. Let dry, if you used glue.

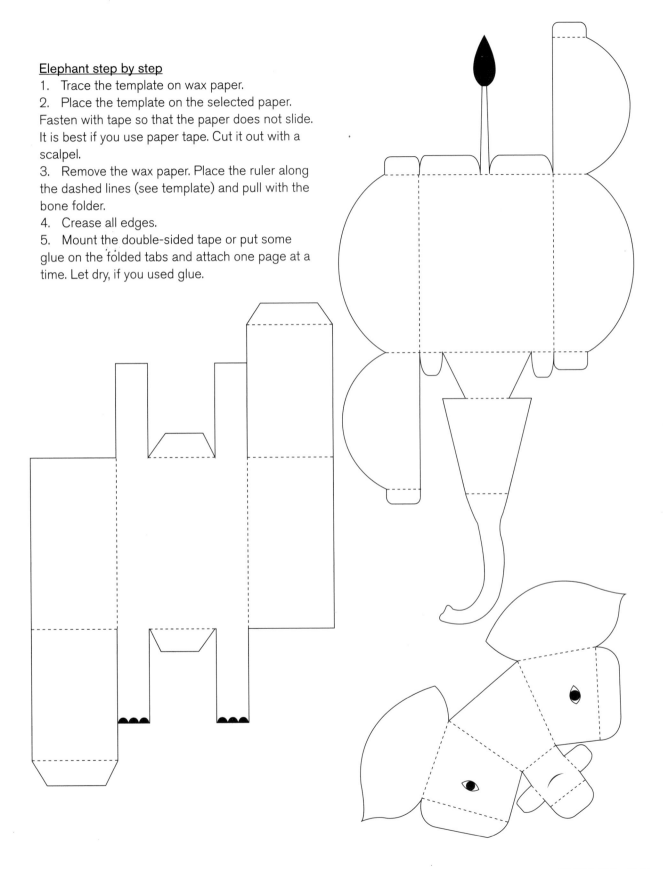

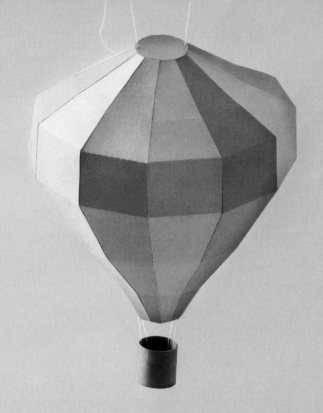

AIR BALLOON

The construction of the air balloon resembles the geometric figures (Refer to pp. 24–33). The difference is that the air balloon is constructed with different geometric shapes, with identical sides and, in addition, they have a completely closed shape.

TOOLS

PAPER

PENCIL

DOUBLE-SIDED TAPE OR GLUE

BONE FOLDER

FOAM BOARD (5MM)

NEEDLE AND THREAD

PAPER TAPE

SCALPEL

WAX PAPER

STEEL RULER

Air balloon step by step

1. Trace the template on page 95 on wax paper 12 times.
2. Choose paper in two colors (of course this works with just one color or multiple colors).
3. Place the templates on the pieces of paper. Fasten with tape so that the paper does not slide. It is best if you use paper tape.
4. Follow the outer lines and cut out 6 parts of each color with a scalpel.
5. Remove the wax paper. Place the ruler along the dashed lines (see template) and pull with the bone folder. Crease all edges.
6. Mount the double-sided tape or glue the folded tabs.
7. Attach the parts in alternating colors until all are attached. Fasten the last tab in the first one to form a round balloon. Let dry, if you used glue.
8. Trace the template for the basket on wax paper and place on your chosen piece of paper.
9. Fasten, cut out, and crease along the dashed line.
10. Use a compass to measure a circle of 0.6" (15 mm) on piece of foamboard, preferably with a thickness of $\frac{3}{16}$" (5 mm), and cut it.
11. Use the double-sided tape or glue around the edge of the circle-shaped foamboard.
12. Place the basket strip around the foamboard so that it creates the edges of the basket. Fasten by removing the protective plastic on the basket tab and let the other side of the strip protrude beyond the glue surface.
13. Trace the circle that is to become the top of the balloon.
14. Place it on one of the colored pieces of paper and cut.
15. Sew through the circle and let the thread come out through the bottom of the balloon.
16. Pull it through the bottom of the basket and let the needle go back on the diagonal side.
17. Put the needle back through the balloon and pull the thread through again at the top of the balloon.
18. Remove the protective plastic on all the tabs making up the top of the balloon and assemble it and the balloon.
19. Now you can control the height of the basket by pulling on the ends of the threads.
20. Make a knot or hang the threads directly on a hook or in a window.

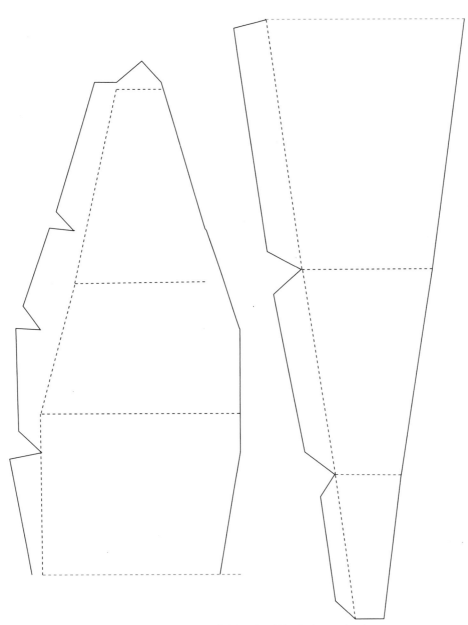

On the air balloon template the red-dashed sides should be facing each other
and together they make up one template. Refer to description on page 93.

x 2 (foamboard +
paper)

Basket template: refer to description on page 93.

animals

A few of my earliest paper constructions were these three animals. It is possible to cut them out in both white and colored paper. If you choose white paper it may be nice to color either the entire animal or certain details.

<u>Zebra and lion step by step</u>
1. Trace the template on wax paper.
2. Place the template on the selected paper. Fasten with tape so that the paper does not slide. It is best if you use paper tape. Cut out with a scalpel.
3. Remove the wax paper. Place the ruler along the dashed lines (see template) and pull with the bone folder.
4. Crease all edges.
5. Mount the double-sided tape or put some glue on the folded tabs and attach one page at a time. Let dry, if you used glue.

Note: Elephant assembly instructions appear on page 91.

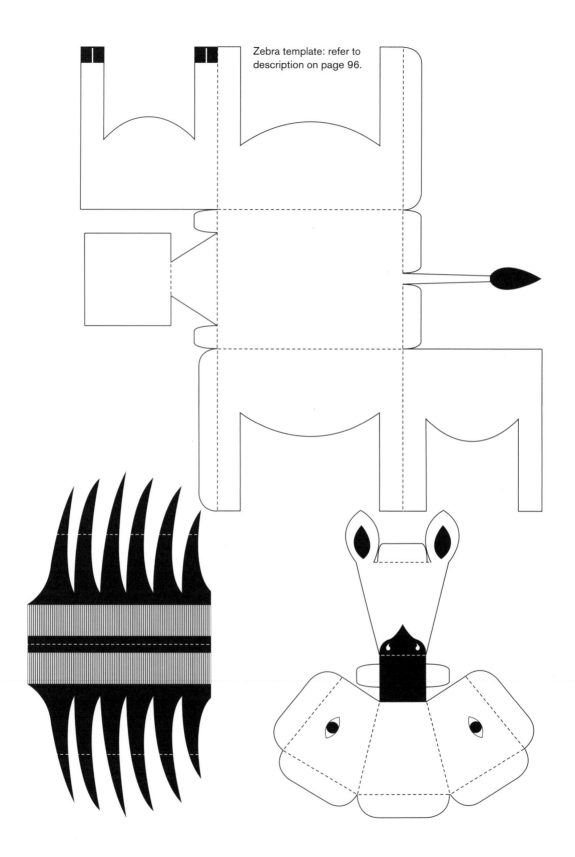

Zebra template: refer to
description on page 96.

Lion template: refer to description on page 96.

buildings

It is possible to vary houses by changing their height, their width, the shape of the roof, or the look of the windows. Here are three houses that are rather similar to each other, but with somewhat different levels of detail. Consider that you can easily add floors to the house, create doors, and add a chimney if you want. Feel free to use a model of a house as a reference point when choosing the color and the shape of the windows.

Christmas display for the Malmsten shop, December 2012.

Houses

When I first arrived at University College of Arts, Crafts and Design, I began making houses out of paper. Since then, it has been a recurring motif, where character and size can be varied. I think that houses can be full of feeling when they are used, both in images and in stories.

Once I built a town in a suitcase, where I mounted a string of lights under the bottom of the suitcase and made holes in the bottom so that every house was lit up by a lamp. Something similar would be fun to test. One way to frame the houses may also be to place them under a glass cover or to arrange them on a window sill.

Houses step by step

1. Trace the house template on wax paper.
2. Place the template on the selected paper. Fasten the wax paper with tape so that the paper does not slide. It is best if you use paper tape.
3. Cut out the windows and any doors with a scalpel. Follow the outer lines and cut out the template.
4. Remove the wax paper. Place the ruler along dashed lines (see template) and pull with the bone folder. Crease all edges.
5. Mount the double-sided tape or glue the folded tabs.
6. Assemble the parts together and let them dry, if you have used glue.
7. Trace the roof template on wax paper.
8. Place the wax paper on the selected paper. Fasten with tape so that the paper does not slide. It is preferable to use paper tape.
9. Follow the outer lines and cut out the template. Remove the wax paper and place the ruler along the dashed lines (see template).
10. Mount the double-sided tape or put some glue on the folded tabs and attach to the house.

TOOLS

PAPER
DOUBLE-SIDED TAPE OR GLUE
BONE FOLDER
PAPER TAPE
SCALPEL
WAX PAPER
STEEL RULER

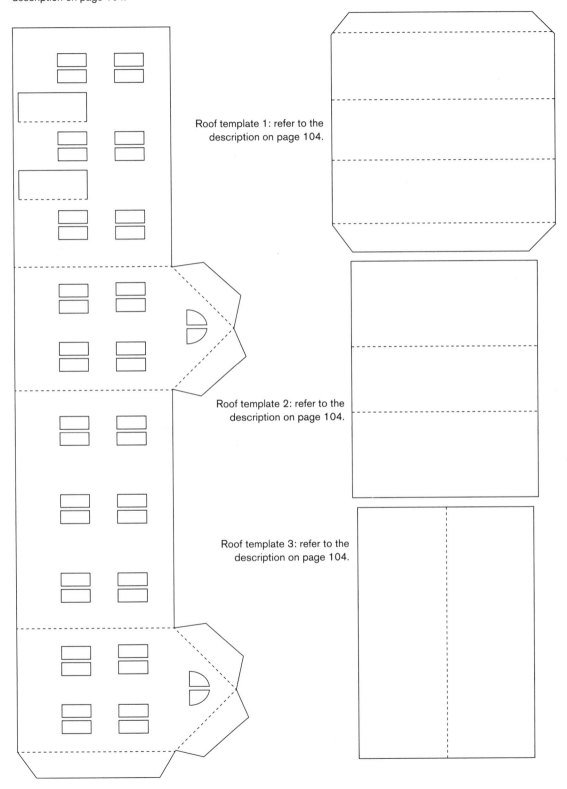

House template 3: refer to the description on page 104.

Roof template 1: refer to the description on page 104.

Roof template 2: refer to the description on page 104.

Roof template 3: refer to the description on page 104.

70 mm

Lighthouse

This is one of my favorite buildings.

I don't know anything as nice as lighthouses.
For so many years they have been a recurring motif in my images and a place I often visit for inspiration.

The environment around the lighthouse usually puts me in a state of mind that is close to the world of imagery and ideas and many projects have had their first impulse from different lighthouse locations.

Lighthouse step by step

1. Trace the template on wax paper.
2. Place the template on the selected paper. Fasten the wax paper with tape so that the paper does not slide. It is best if you use paper tape.
3. Follow the outer lines and cut out the template with a scalpel.
4. Remove the wax paper. Place the ruler along the dashed lines (see template) and pull with the bone folder. Crease all edges.
5. Mount the double-sided tape or glue the folded tabs.
6. Mount the bottom plate and the upper plate in the lighthouse tower so that the tower is stable and keeps its shape.
7. Assemble the parts and fasten them together. Let dry, if you used glue.

SCALE 1:2

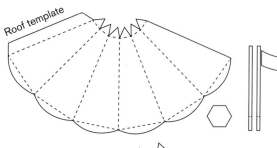

Roof template

Lighthouse tower template

Inner fence template

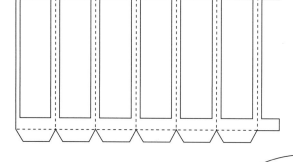

Upper floor lighthouse (foamboard) template

Bottom floor, outer fence (foamboard + paper) template

Bottom floor lighthouse (foamboard) template

Outer fence template

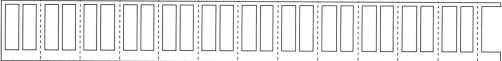

TOOLS
PAPER
PENCIL
DOUBLE-SIDED TAPE OR GLUE
BONE FOLDER
FOAM BOARD ³/₁₆" (5 MM)
PAPER TAPE
SCALPEL
WAX PAPER
STEEL RULER

inspiration

Here are a few examples of images of different projects that I have done. I work about the same amount with international clients as with Swedish ones. When I receive a job I start by making detailed sketches in Illustrator. That way I can easily test different compositions, sizes, and color combinations.

By using this method it is easy to discuss the idea and how it should be designed with those involved in the project. After the sketch is approved I can start cutting and building in a concentrated fashion.

Most of the objects I build are made from A4 sheets of paper and they do not end up being very large. The completed sets usually fit on a worktable, which makes it practical when they are to be transported to a photo studio for arrangement and lighting. On site in the studio where the image is constructed, the objects are hung by threads or mounted in place. I like leaving the sewing threads visible in the final result. They strengthen the papery and tactile feel of the technique.

The assignments and my own projects that consist of a series of images are those that I like the best. To get to work in a narrative fashion, design characters, and have their gazes and body language "perform" is a little bit like me climbing into the world of imagery and, like a marionette maker, compose and create ambiance and images. It is amazingly fun.

My own project where I have constructed a pop-up directly in a newspaper spread that I then mounted in a book.

Examples of images from a project I did for ibis Styles.
The left image symbolizes business and the right one is all-inclusive.

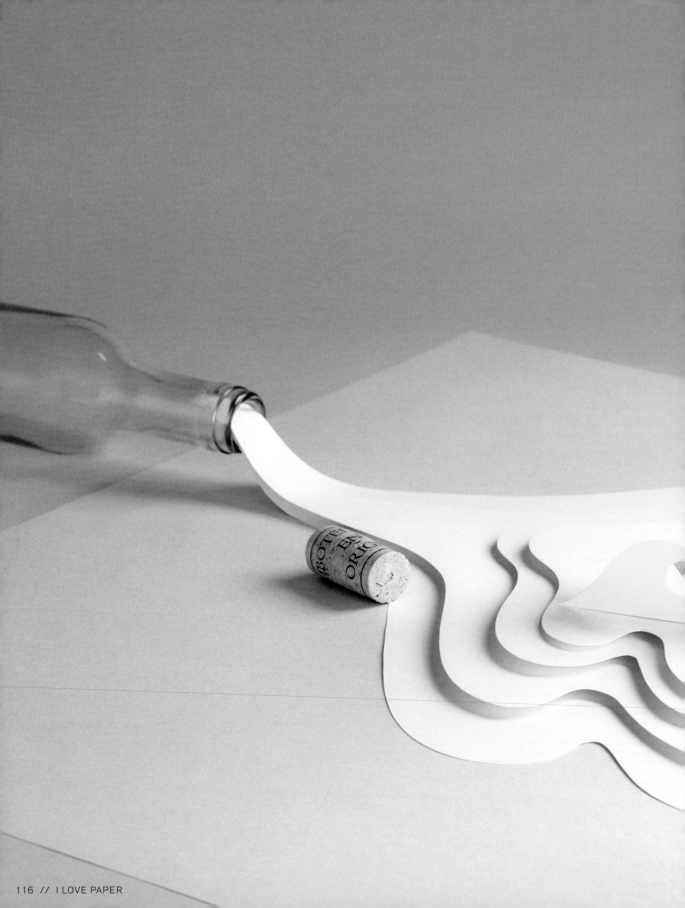

your own notes

You are welcome to write or draw ideas here that
you want to create out of paper.

thanks!

There are very many people that I would like to thank now that I have the chance. First, it almost filled a sheet of paper, but then I decided to be brief instead. I believe you know who you are and how infinitely much I care about you. Thank you for being there and I hope that everything remains wonderful for you!

♥-felt thank you to Maria Wretblad who took most of the photos for this book. The images are from a close and fun cooperation that has evolved between Maria and me. Also thank you to Aril Wretblad who has helped out by illuminating everything so nicely.

Hooray for paper!

Campaign image for Kronans Droghandel.

about the author

Fideli Sundqvist graduated from University College of Arts, Crafts and Design in 2011, and has worked as a paper cutter full time since then. In addition to advertising and display jobs around the world, she has also had her own exhibitions.